I'm Reading About

PENNSYLVANIA

The Keystone State!

GALLOPADE

by Carole Marsh

Printed and Manufactured in Peachtree City, GA., USA
www.gallopade.com

Book design: John Hanson

Editorial manager: Janice Baker

Pennsylvania is a great state.

It is one of a kind.

What makes Pennsylvania special?

Let's read about it and see!

NATIVE AMERICANS

Who lived in Pennsylvania first?

Native Americans did!

They moved around to find food.
They hunted in Pennsylvania's woods.
They fished in Pennsylvania's rivers.
They gathered fruits and seeds and nuts.

EXPLORERS

Some explorers came to
Pennsylvania in 1609.
They came from the country of Holland.

Henry Hudson was their leader.
He and his men sailed up Delaware Bay.
They claimed the area for Holland!

SETTLEMENT

A man named William Penn came from England to America. He started the first settlement in Pennsylvania. He named it Philadelphia.

William Penn settled Philadelphia with a group of people called Quakers.

Philadelphia

STATEHOOD

Pennsylvania was the second state to join the United States of America!

Isn't it great,
to be a state!
I bet Pennsylvania
could hardly wait!

Pennsylvania became a state in 1787.

Pennsylvania
The 2nd State
Here we are!

FLAG

I am the state flag.
I was adopted in 1907.

What color am I?
I am blue.

Look at me.
What else do you see?

I fly high over the state of Pennsylvania!

VIRTUE
LIBERTY AND
INDEPENDENCE

CAPITAL

Say hello to Harrisburg,
the capital city of Pennsylvania!

There is an important building in Harrisburg.
It is the State Capitol.
Pennsylvania's laws are made there!

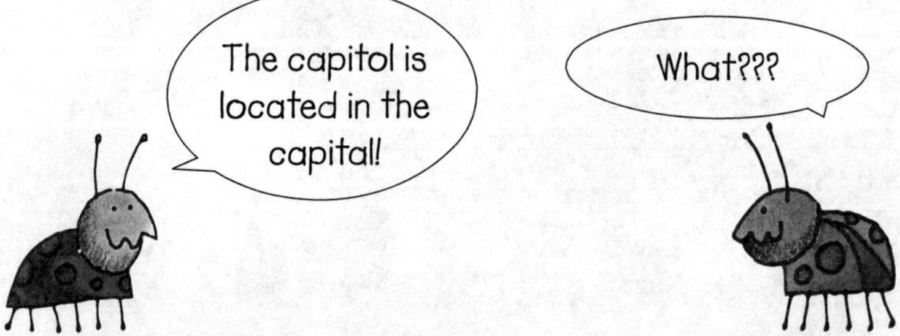

Capitol

SEAL

I am a seal,
but I am not the State Seal.
If I were, I would be very important.
I would be stamped on many official papers.
(Ouch, that might hurt!)

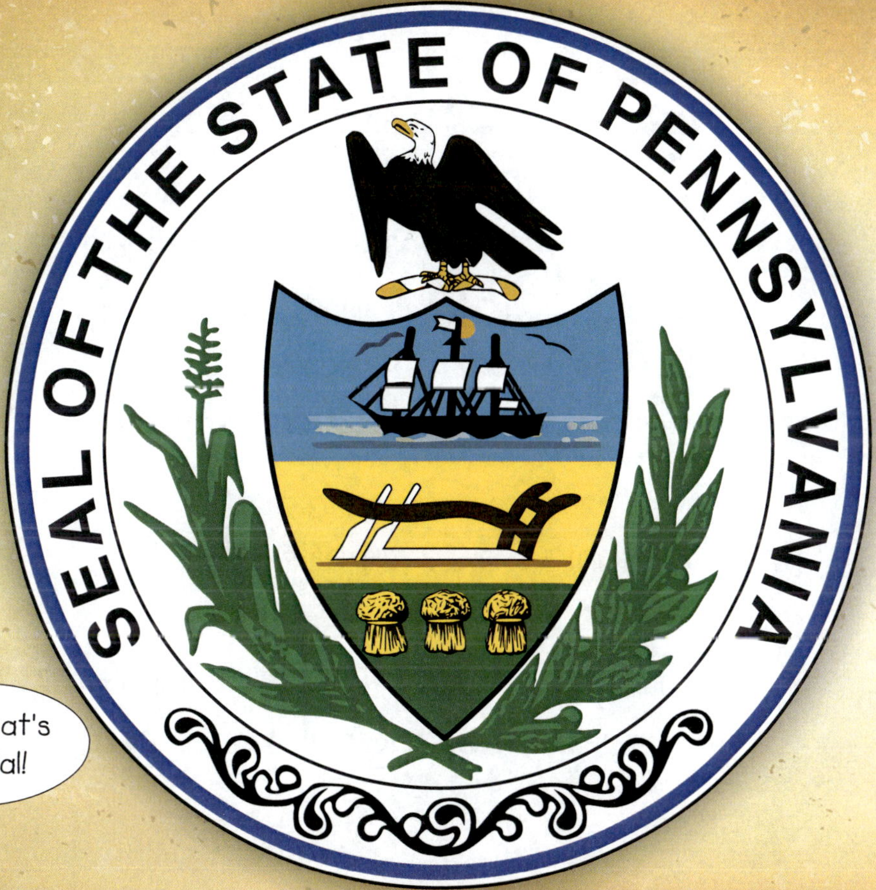
SEAL OF THE STATE OF PENNSYLVANIA

Now, that's official!

NICKNAME

State nicknames are fun!
State nicknames are great!
They share fun facts
about each state!

Pennsylvania's nickname is "The Keystone State."

Pennsylvania is located in the middle
of the original 13 colonies.

The Keystone State

BORDERS

Look at Pennsylvania.
Pennsylvania is in a region called "the Northeast."

Pennsylvania borders six other states.

Pennsylvania means "Penn's Woods." It was named for William Penn.

Borders

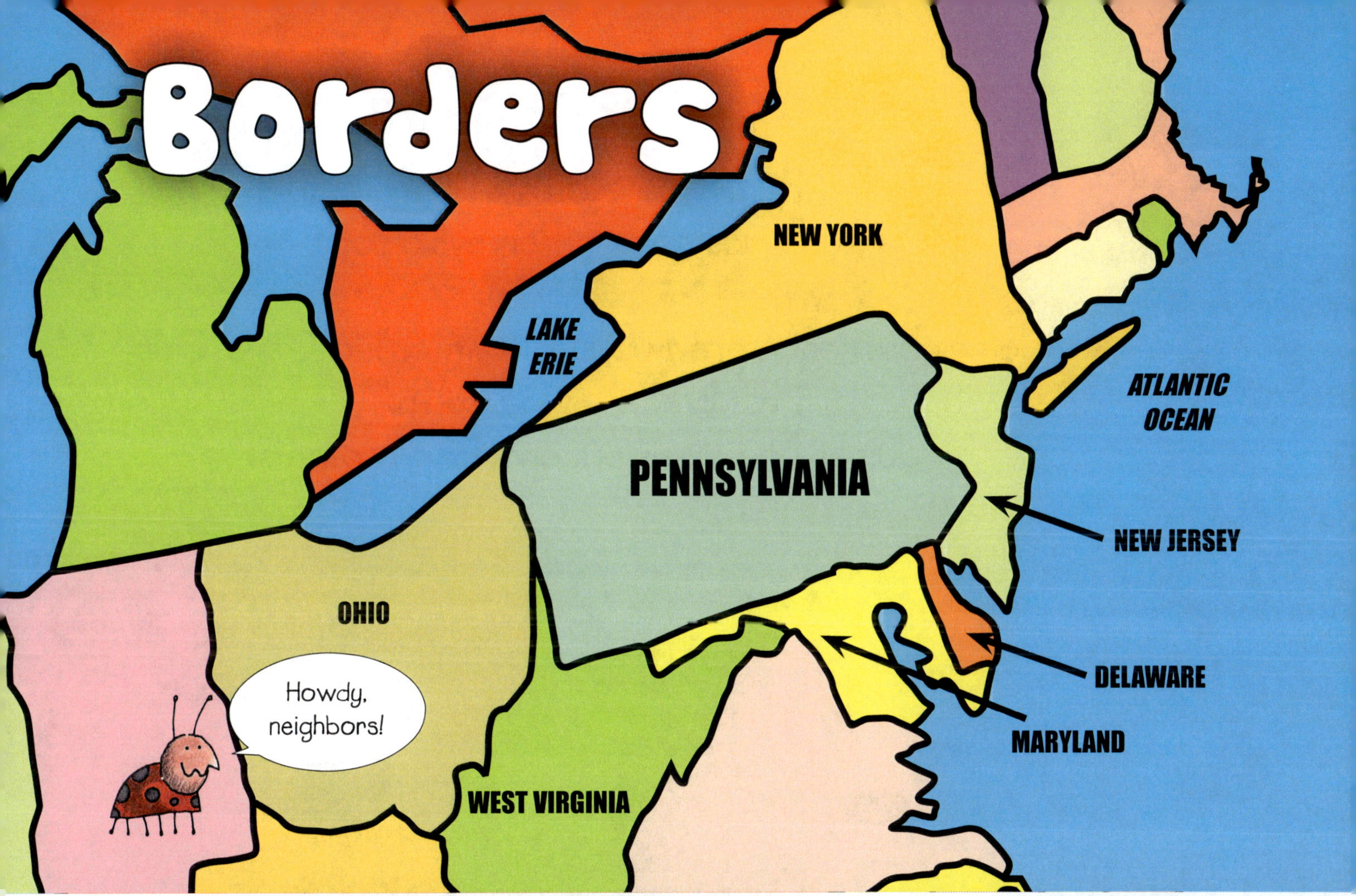
NEW YORK
LAKE
ERIE
ATLANTIC
OCEAN
PENNSYLVANIA
NEW JERSEY
OHIO
DELAWARE
MARYLAND
WEST VIRGINIA
Howdy,
neighbors!

PRESIDENT

James Buchanan was the 15th President
of the United States of America.
He was born in Pennsylvania!

James Buchanan grew up in a town called Cove Gap.
His lived in a log cabin.
James had six sisters and four brothers!

James Buchanan

PEOPLE

Many famous people

Benjamin Franklin

Founding Father of the United States

Daniel Boone

Explorer and frontiersman

Louisa May Alcott

Author of the book *Little Women*

call our state home!

Milton Hershey
Founder of the Hershey Chocolate Company

Joe Biden
U.S. Vice President under President Barack Obama

Guion Bluford
First African American astronaut in space

PEOPLE

Ruffed Grouse

I am the state game bird, and I fly
over Pennsylvania, proud and high.

As I fly, up in the sky,
I flap my wings to tell you "Hi!"

The Pennsylvania state game bird
is the Ruffed Grouse.

GAME BIRD

Mountain Laurel

FLOWER

I am the Mountain Laurel.
I am the state flower.

I grow where it's warm and sunny.
I bloom in the spring and summer.
I help make Pennsylvania beautiful!

Look at me! Smell me!
My blooms are white and pink!

Hemlock

TREE

I am a Hemlock—I'm the state tree.
All over Pennsylvania is where to find me.

My roots run deep, they keep me strong.
My leaves stay green, all year long.

I stand up straight, big and tall.
Don't climb too high—it would hurt to fall!

Firefly

INSECT

I am the Firefly.
I am the state insect.

You can spot me at night.
My tail glows in the dark!

I am a type of beetle.
Many people call me a "lightning bug."

Lakes

Let's go to the lake!

We can wade in the water.
We can ride on a boat.

We can jump off the dock
onto an inner tube float!

Lake Erie, Pennsylvania's Great Lake,
is home to many animals:

Fish Snakes Birds Turtles Salamanders and More!

LAKES

Allegheny Mountains

MOUNTAINS

Pennsylvania's Allegheny Mountains
are the place to be.
Hiking, fishing, camping—
fun for you and me.

If you were to climb
to the top of a tree,
you'd have a very nice view to see!

Rivers

RIVERS

Pennsylvania has many rivers.
People like to use rivers for boating and fishing!

This habitat is home to many animals:

Birds Deer Snakes Frogs Fish and More!

Many of Pennsylvania's early settlers built towns along rivers.

Did you hear the one about the Liberty Bell?
Yeah! It cracked me up!
Liberty Bell

LANDMARK

The Liberty Bell is a large metal bell.
It is located in the city of Philadelphia.

The Liberty Bell rang to announce important events in American history.
It is a symbol of America's freedom!

A long crack runs down the middle of the bell.

Pennsylvania Crops

AGRICULTURE

Pennsylvania has many farms.
Why?
Because Pennsylvania has good soil and a mild climate!

Some of the top crops grown in Pennsylvania are:

Corn **Mushrooms** **Soybeans** **Apples**

Hey!
Don't forget about me!
I am a Pennsylvania cow.
I produce lots of milk
to make dairy products!
Mooooooooooo!

Sports in Pennsylvania

SPORTS

Baseball! Basketball! Football! Hockey!
Pennsylvania has it all.

Whether you like to watch or play,
You are sure to have a ball!

Pirates **Phillies** **76ers**

Flyers

Steelers **Eagles**

Penguins

Nittany Lions

Panthers **& More!**

Pennsylvania: Home of Crayola Crayons

Crayola crayons were invented by two cousins.
Their first box had just eight crayons.
The colors were:

Black	**Brown**	**Blue**	**Red**
Purple	**Orange**	**Yellow**	**Green**

You can visit the Crayola Experience in Easton!

GLOSSARY

astronaut: a person trained to travel in space

author: person who writes a book, article, or other text

climate: weather conditions in an area over a long period of time

elect: to choose someone by voting

Founding Father: a person who helped form the United States as a nation

frontiersman: a person who lives on new, unsettled land

habitat: a place where plants or animals naturally live

laws: rules made by the government

region: an area that has similar characteristics

settlement: the first community in an area